THE LIBRARY OF
SHOWTUNES

ISBN: 978-1-78038-905-9

Visit Hal Leonard Online at
www.halleonard.com

Contact us:
Hal Leonard
7777 West Bluemound Road
Milwaukee, WI 53213
Email: info@halleonard.com

In Europe, contact:
Hal Leonard Europe Limited
42 Wigmore Street
Marylebone, London, W1U 2RY
Email: info@halleonardeurope.com

In Australia, contact:
Hal Leonard Australia Pty. Ltd.
4 Lentara Court
Cheltenham, Victoria, 3192 Australia
Email: info@halleonard.com.au

THE LIBRARY OF
SHOWTUNES

Contents

All I Ask Of You

from The Phantom Of The Opera

Music by Andrew Lloyd Webber
Lyrics by Charles Hart
Additional Lyrics by Richard Stilgoe

No more talk of dark-ness, for- -get these wide-eyed fears; I'm here, no-thing can harm you, my words will warm and calm you. Let me be your free-dom, let day-light dry your tears; I'm

here, with you, be-side you, to guard you and to guide you.

Say you love me ev-'ry wak-ing mo-ment, turn my head with talk of

sum-mer-time. Say you need me with you now and al-ways;

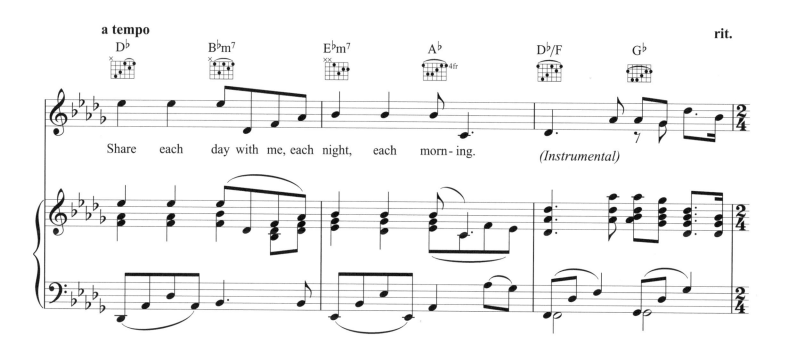

Share each day with me, each night, each morn-ing.

(Instrumental)

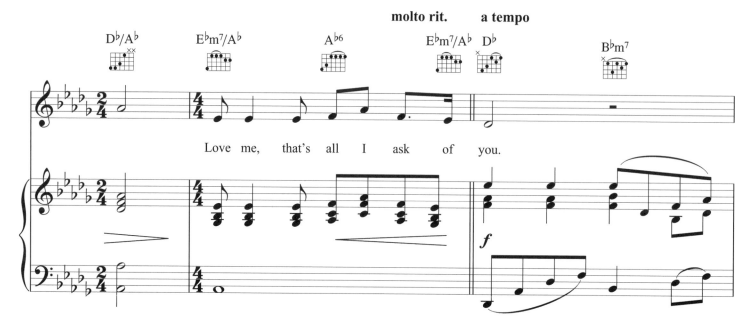

Love me, that's all I ask of you.

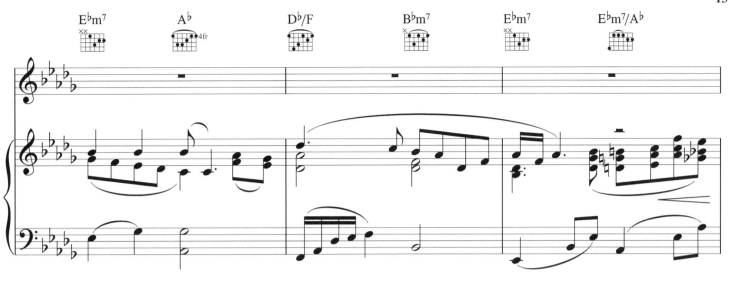

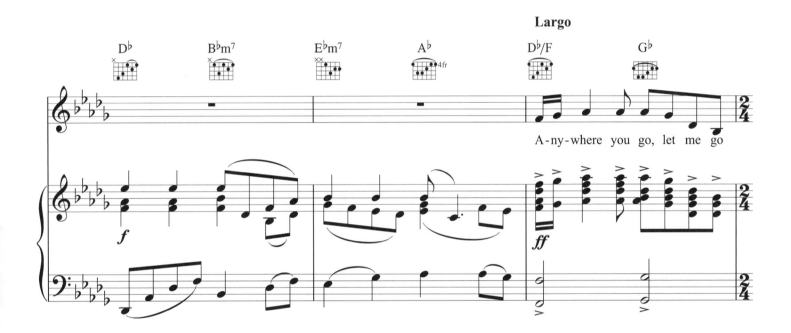

Largo

A-ny-where you go, let me go

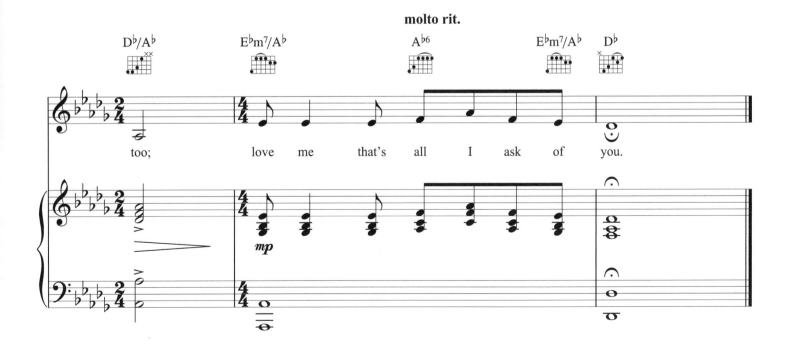

molto rit.

too; love me that's all I ask of you.

Aquarius

from Hair

Words by James Rado & Gerome Ragni
Music by Galt MacDermot

-qua - ri - us, A -

-qua - ri - us.

Har - mo - ny and un - der - stand - ing, Sym - pa - thy and trust a - bound-

- ing. No more false-hoods or de - ri - sions, Gold - en

As Long As He Needs Me

from Oliver!

Words & Music by Lionel Bart

Big Spender

from Sweet Charity

Words by Dorothy Fields
Music by Cy Coleman

Bring Him Home

from Les Misérables

Music by Claude-Michel Schönberg
Lyrics by Alain Boublil & Herbert Kretzmer

But Not For Me

from Girl Crazy

Words & Music by George Gershwin & Ira Gershwin

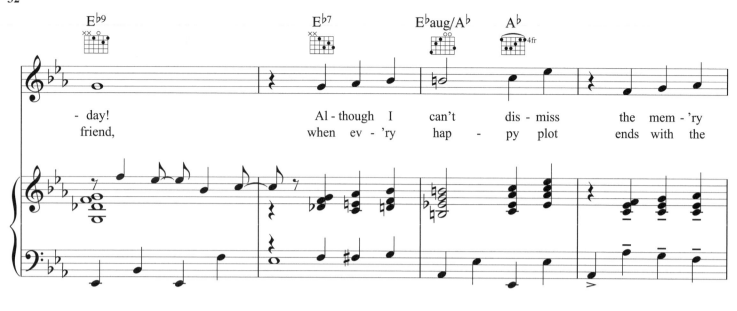

-day!
friend,

Al - though I can't dis - miss the mem - 'ry
when ev - 'ry hap - py plot ends with the

of his kiss, I guess he's not for
mar - riage knot, and there's no knot for

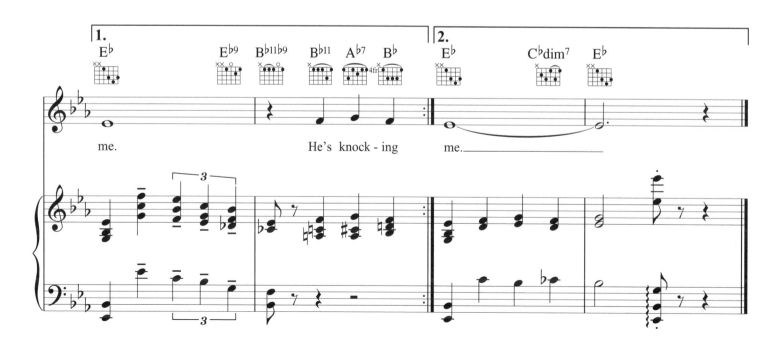

me.
He's knock - ing me.

Cabaret

from Cabaret

Words by Fred Ebb
Music by John Kander

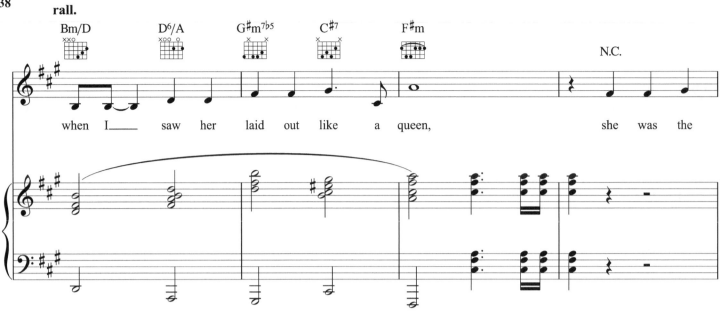

when I___ saw her laid out like a queen, she was the

hap-pi-est corpse I'd ev-er seen._____ I

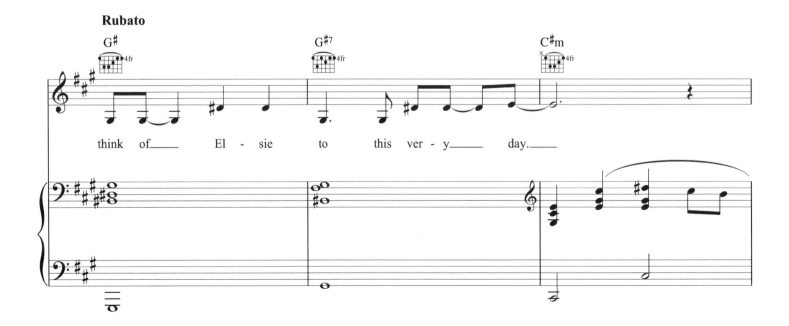

think of___ El-sie to this ver-y___ day.___

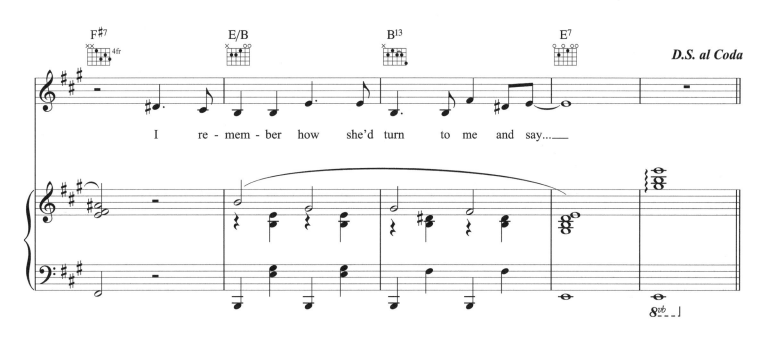

I re - mem - ber how she'd turn to me and say....___

But as for me, but as for me,

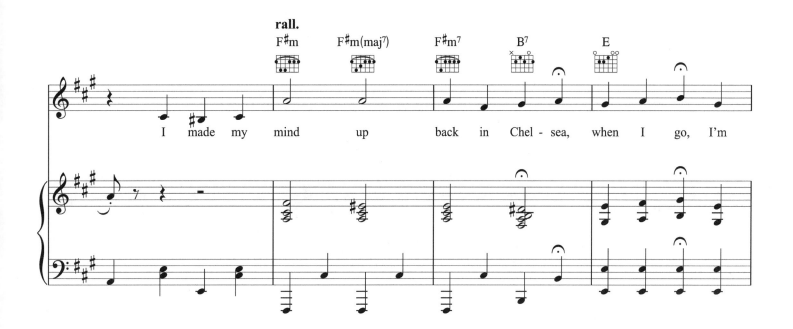

I made my mind up back in Chel - sea, when I go, I'm

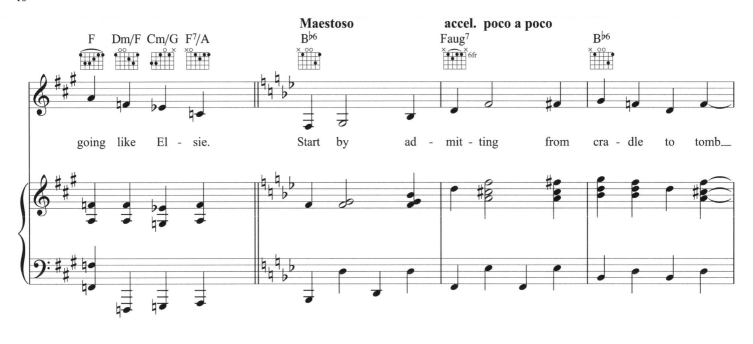

going like El - sie. Start by ad - mit - ting from cra - dle to tomb

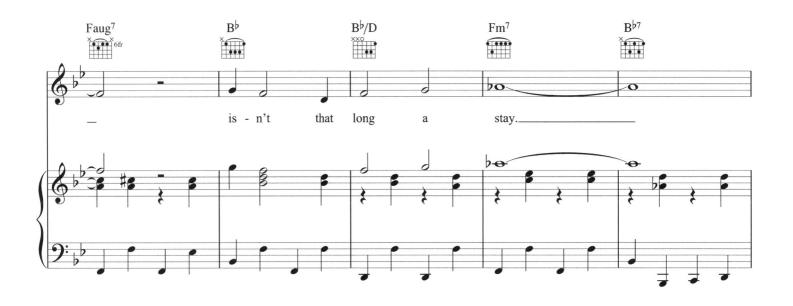

— is - n't that long a stay.

Life is a cab - a - ret, old chum,

Can You Feel The Love Tonight

from The Lion King

Words by Tim Rice
Music by Elton John

1. There's a calm surrender to the rush of day, when the heat of the rolling world

To Coda ⊕

kings___ and___ va-ga-bonds be-lieve the ve-ry best.___

2. There's a time___ for ev-'ry-one, if they on-ly learn___

that the twist-ing ka-lei-do-scope___ moves us all___ in turn.___

There's a rhyme and rea - son to the wild out-doors when the heart of this star- crossed voy- ag - er

D.S al Coda   ⊕ CODA

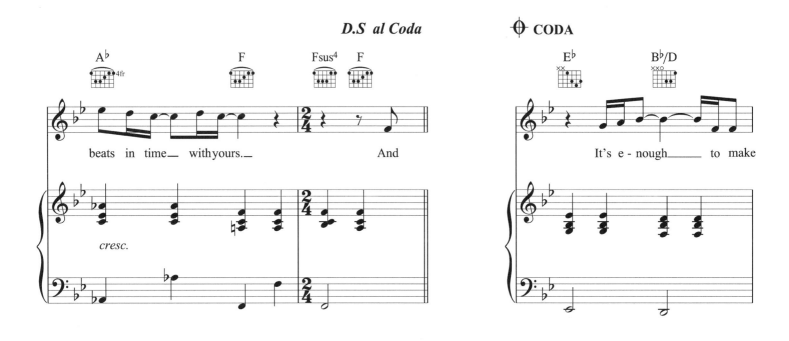

beats in time__ with yours.__   And

It's e - nough_____ to make

cresc.

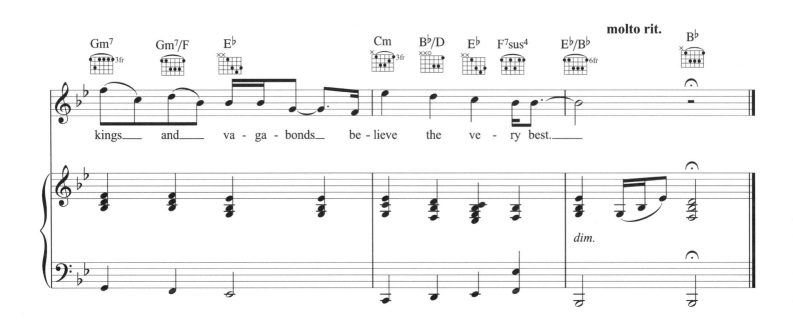

kings__ and__ va - ga - bonds__ be - lieve the ve - ry best.__

dim.   **molto rit.**

Can't Help Lovin' Dat Man

from Show Boat

Words by Oscar Hammerstein II
Music by Jerome Kern

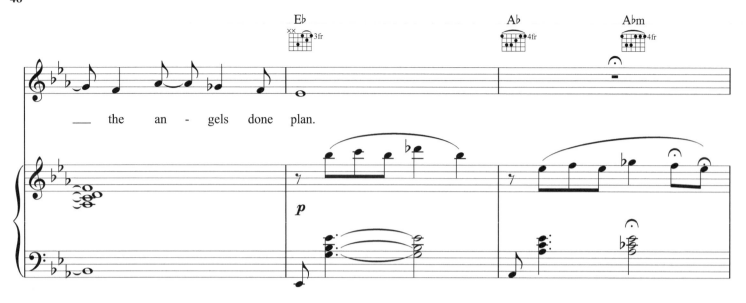

the an - gels done plan.

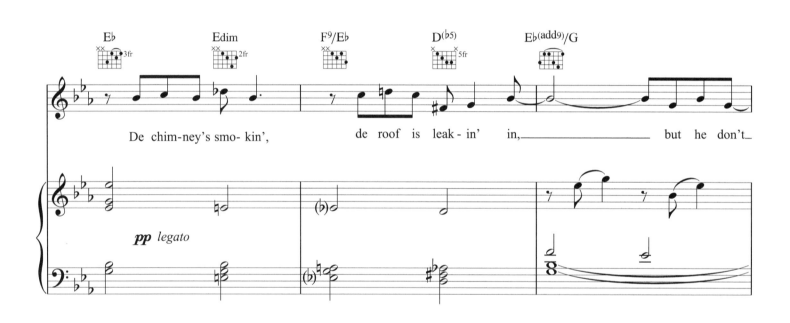

De chim-ney's smo-kin', de roof is leak-in' in,_____ but he don't_

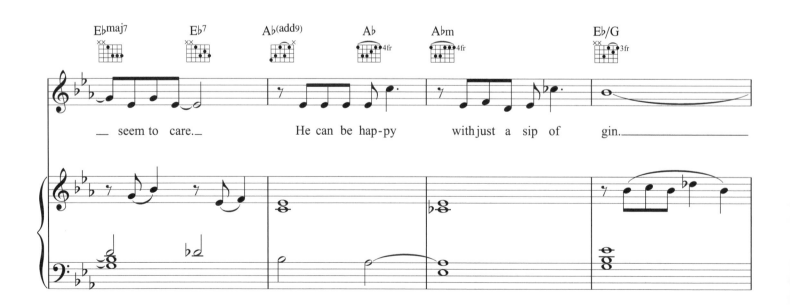

_ seem to care._ He can be hap-py with just a sip of gin._

I e-ven loves him when___ his kiss-es got

gin!

Fish got-ta swim,_____ and

birds___ got-ta fly;___ I got-ta love_____ one man___ till I die.___

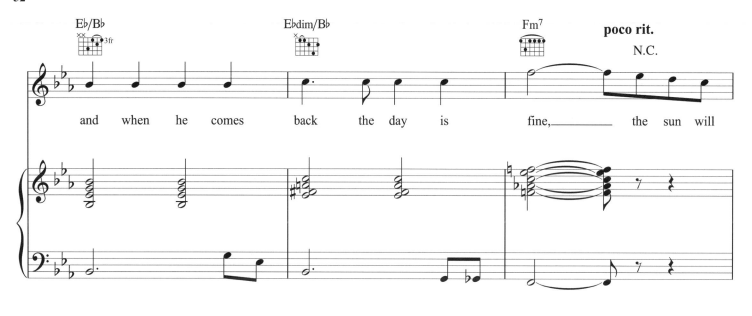

and when he comes back the day is fine, _____ the sun will

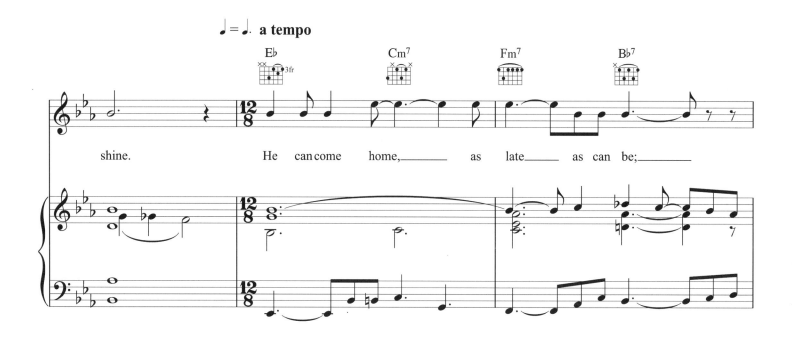

shine. He can come home, _____ as late _____ as can be; _____

Home with-out him _____ ain't no home to me. _____ Can't help

Can't Take My Eyes Off You

from Jersey Boys

Words & Music by Bob Crewe & Bob Gaudio

Verse 3:

You're just too good to be true
Can't take my eyes off you
You'd be like heaven to touch
I wanna hold you so much
At long last love has arrived
And I thank God I'm alive
You're just too good to be true
Can't take my eyes off you.

I love you baby *etc.*

Chim Chim Cher-ee

from Mary Poppins

Words & Music by Richard M. Sherman & Robert B. Sherman

Prologue version:
Room 'ere for everyone, gather round
The constable's responsable! Now, 'ow does that sound?
Ullo, Miss Lark, I've got one for you
Miss Lark love to "wark" in the park with Andrew!
Ah, Missus Corey, a story for you
Your daughters were shorter than you, but they grew!
Dear Miss Persimmon, – (*pause*) – winds in the east – there's a mist coming in
Like something is brewing and 'bout to begin
Can't put my finger on what lies in store
But I feel what's to 'appen all 'appened before.

The "Sidewalk Artist" version:
Chim chiminey, chim chiminey, chim chim cheroo!
I does what I likes and I likes what I do
Today I'm a screever and as you can see
A screever's an artist of 'ighest degree
And it's all me own work from me own memory
Chim chiminey, chim chiminey, chim chim cheroo!
I drawers what I likes and I likes what I drew
No remuneration do I ask of you
But me cap would be glad of a copper or two
Me cap would be glad of a copper or two.

Close Every Door

from Joseph And The Amazing Technicolor® Dreamcoat

Music by Andrew Lloyd Webber

Lyrics by Tim Rice

Consider Yourself

from Oliver!

Words & Music by Lionel Bart

Dancing Queen

from Mamma Mia!

Words & Music by Benny Andersson,
Stig Anderson & Björn Ulvaeus

Defying Gravity

from Wicked

Words & Music by Stephen Schwartz

Don't Cry For Me Argentina

from Evita

Music by Andrew Lloyd Webber
Lyrics by Tim Rice

look at me to know that ev-'ry word is true.

Electricity

from Billy Elliot

Words by Lee Hall
Music by Elton John

♩ = 68

1. I can't real-ly ex-plain it, I have-n't got the words.__ It's a
(2.) bit like be-ing an-gry, it's a bit like be-ing scared,__ con-
feel-ing that you can't con-trol.____ I sup-
-fused and all mixed up and mad as hell.____ It's

Everything's Coming Up Roses

from Gypsy

Words by Stephen Sondheim
Music by Jule Styne

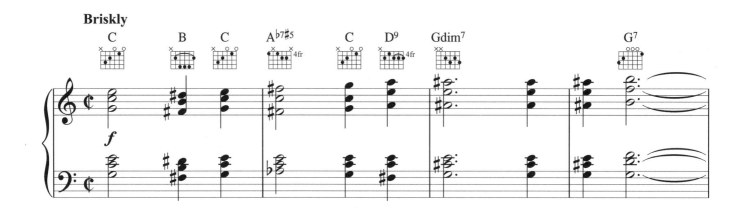

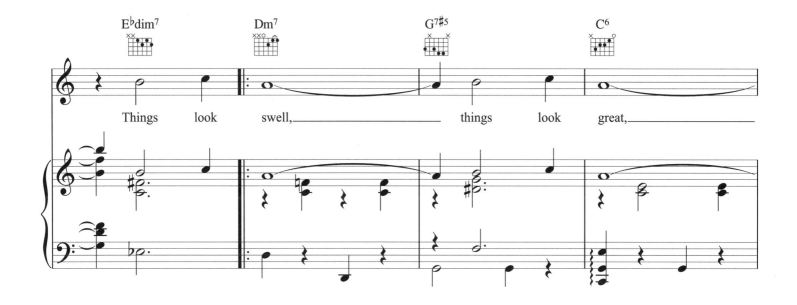

Things look swell,_____ things look great,_____

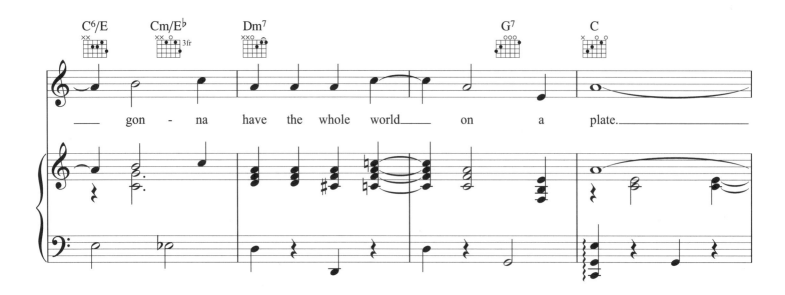

___ gon - na have the whole world___ on a plate._____

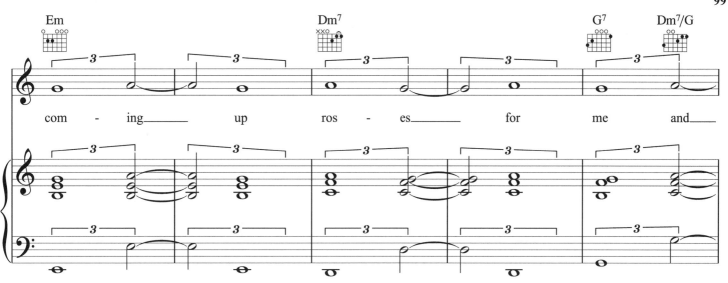

com - ing_____ up ros - es_____ for me and_____

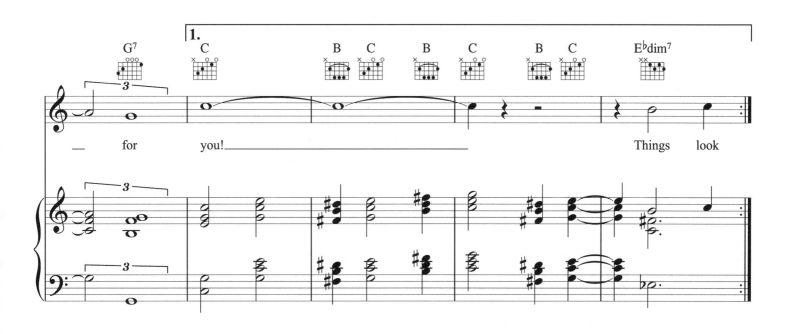

_____ for you!_____ Things look

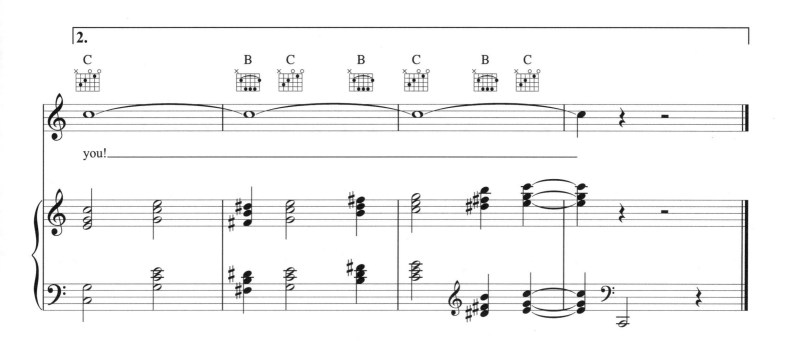

you!_____

Food, Glorious Food

from Oliver!

Words & Music by Lionel Bart

gru - el! There's not a crust; not a crumb can we find, can we

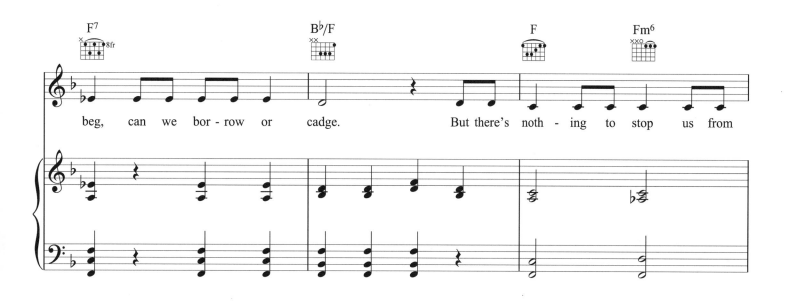

beg, can we bor - row or cadge. But there's noth - ing to stop us from

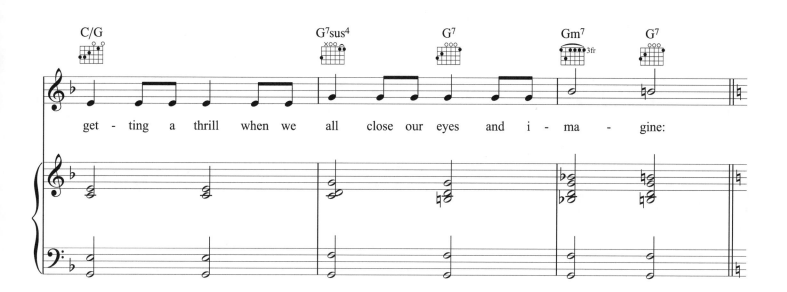

get - ting a thrill when we all close our eyes and i - ma - gine:

♩ = 70

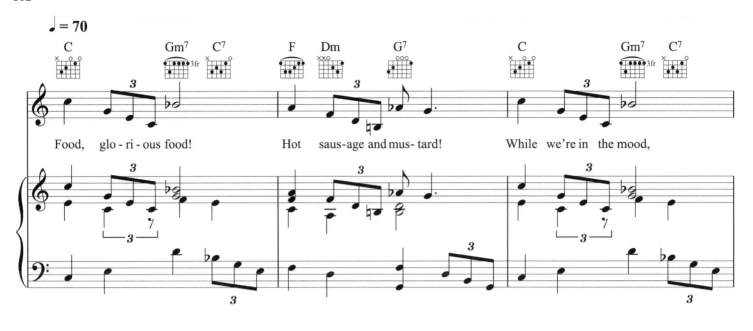

Food, glo - ri - ous food! Hot saus-age and mus- tard! While we're in the mood,

cold jel - ly and cus- tard! Pease pud - ding and sa - ve - loys.

"What next?" is the ques - tion. Rich gen - tle-men have it, boys: in - dye - ges - tion!

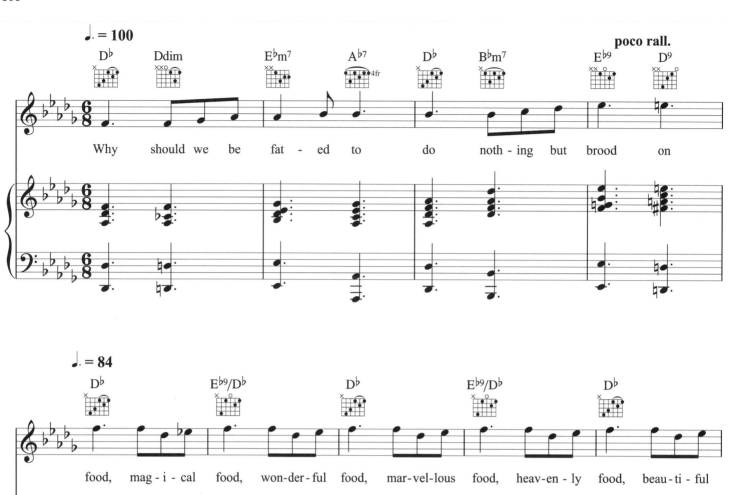

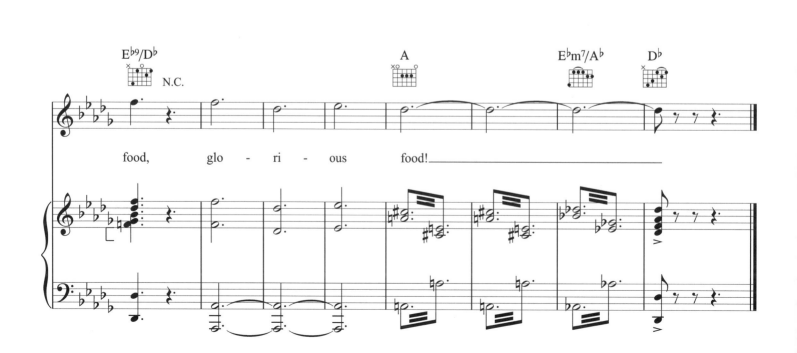

Footloose

from Footloose

Words & Music by Kenny Loggins & Dean Pitchford

Coda ⊕

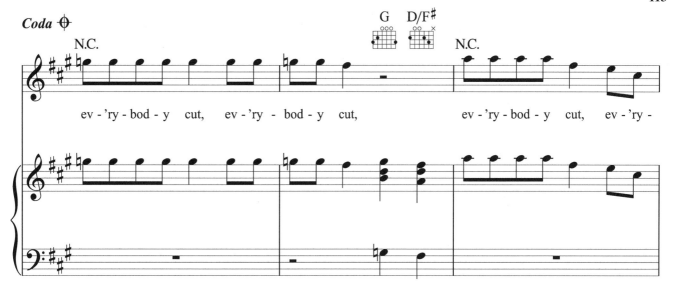

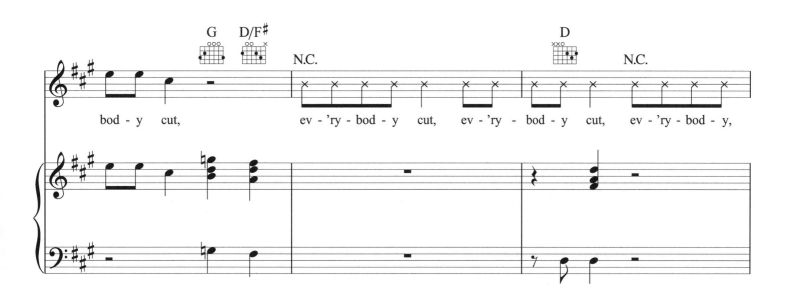

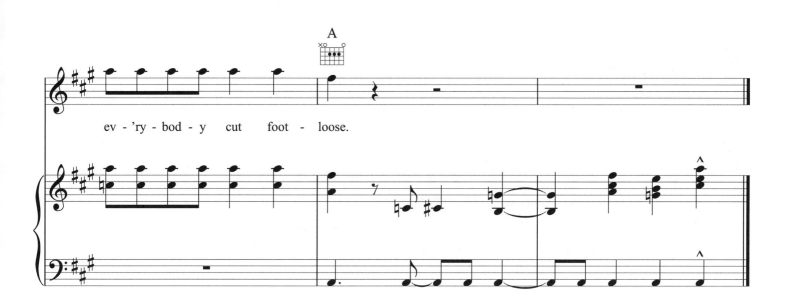

Good Morning Baltimore

from Hairspray

Words & Music by Marc Shaiman & Scott Wittman

Medium '60s Rock

Oh, oh, oh. Woke up to - day
Oh, oh, oh. Look at my hair. What

feel - ing the way I al - ways do, Oh, oh, oh.
"do" can com - pare with mine to - day? Oh, oh, oh.

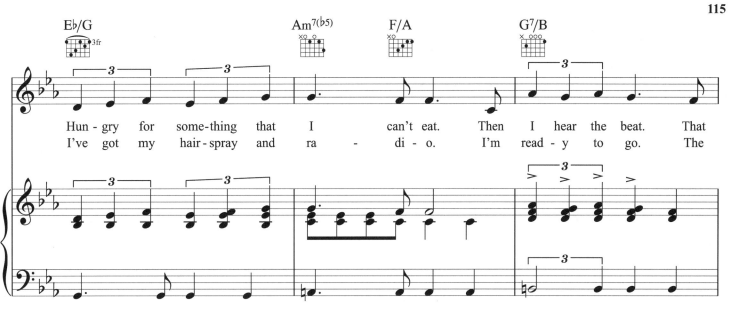

Hun - gry for some-thing that I can't eat. Then I hear the beat. That
I've got my hair-spray and ra - di - o. I'm read - y to go. The

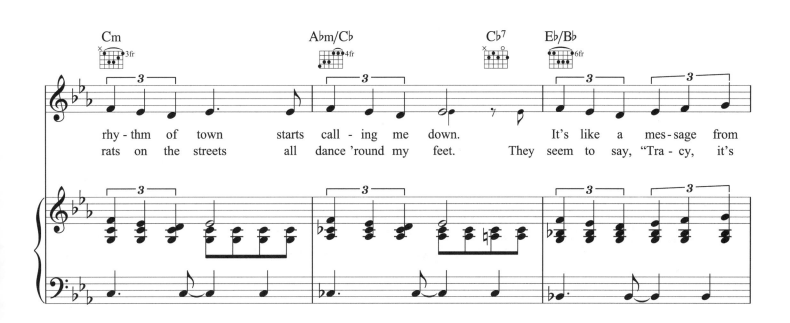

rhy - thm of town starts call - ing me down. It's like a mes - sage from
rats on the streets all dance 'round my feet. They seem to say, "Tra - cy, it's

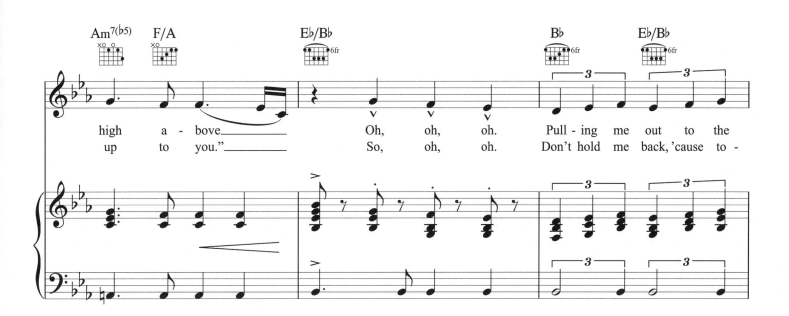

high a - bove___ Oh, oh, oh. Pull - ing me out to the
up to you."___ So, oh, oh. Don't hold me back, 'cause to -

2.

me. I know ev-'ry step. I

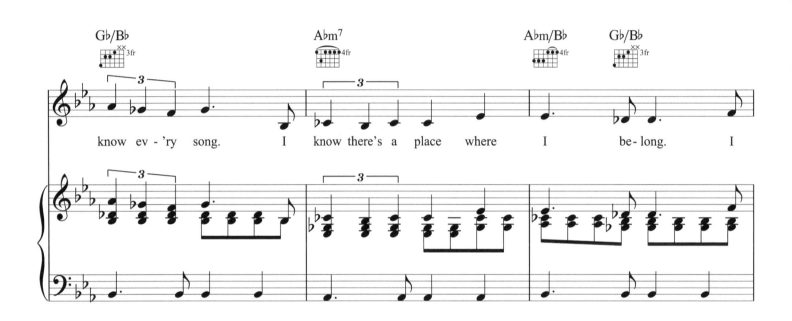

know ev-'ry song. I know there's a place where I be-long. I

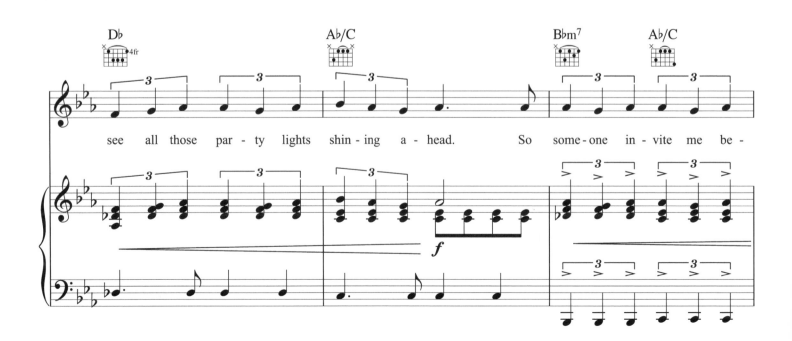

see all those par-ty lights shin-ing a-head. So some-one in-vite me be-

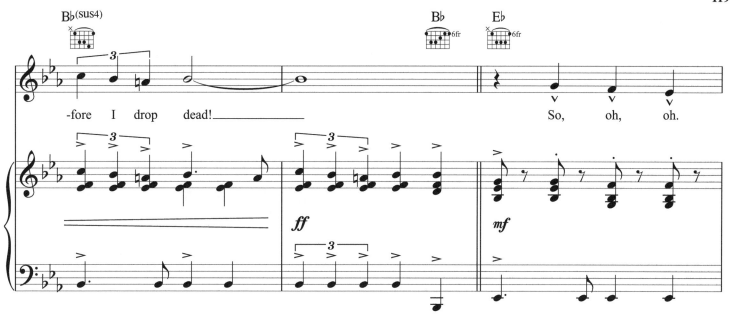

-fore I drop dead!_____ So, oh, oh.

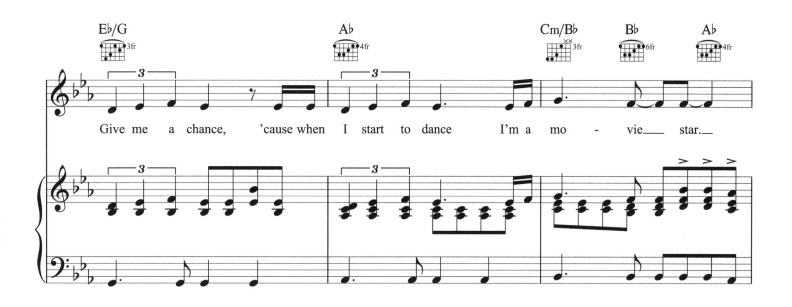

Give me a chance, 'cause when I start to dance I'm a mo - vie___ star.___

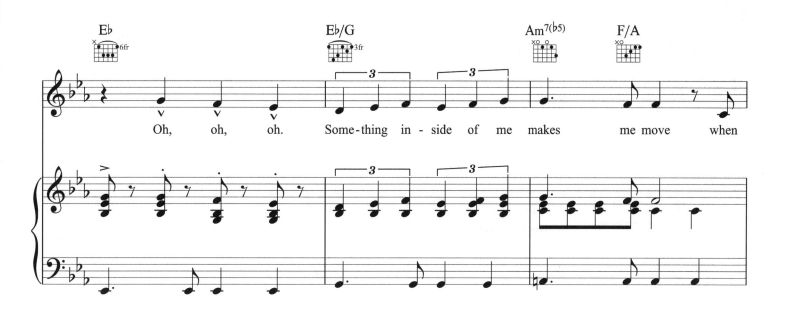

Oh, oh, oh. Some-thing in - side of me makes me move when

I hear the groove. My ma tells me, "No,"_____ but my feet tell me, "Go."

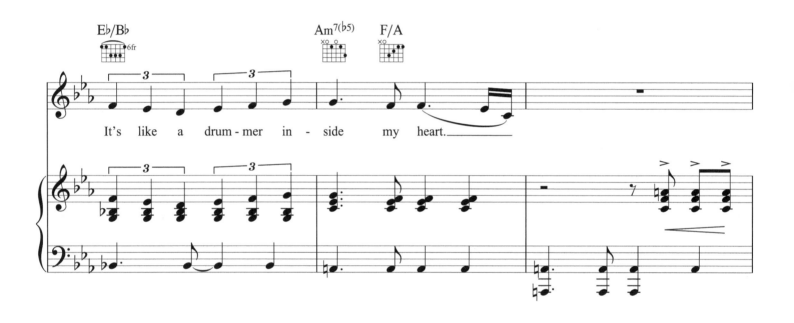

It's like a drum-mer in-side my heart._____

Oh, oh, oh. Don't make me wait one more mo-ment for my life to

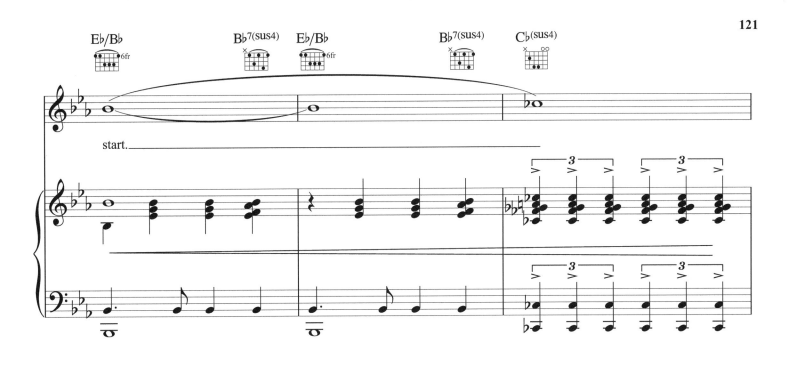

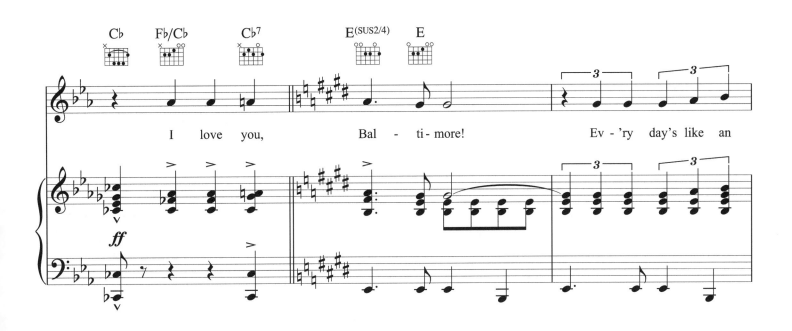

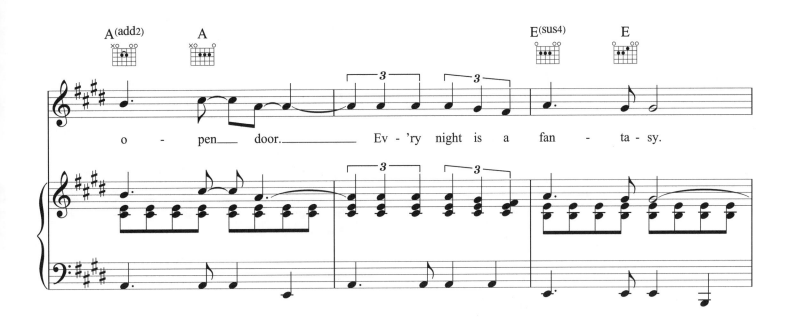

Ev - 'ry sound's like a sym - pho - ny. And I prom - ise,

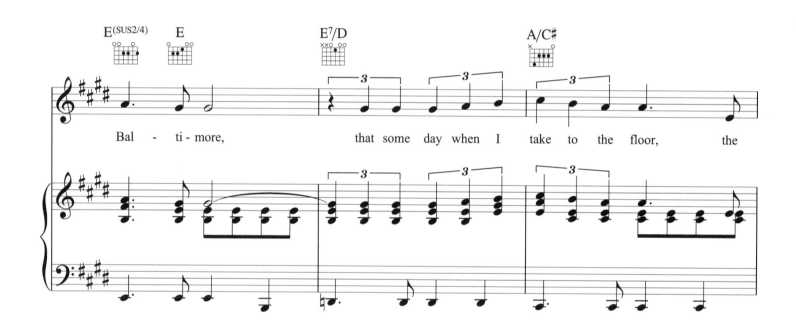

Bal - ti - more, that some day when I take to the floor, the

world's gon - na wake up___ and___ see,

42nd Street

from 42nd Street

Words & Music by Al Dubin & Harry Warren

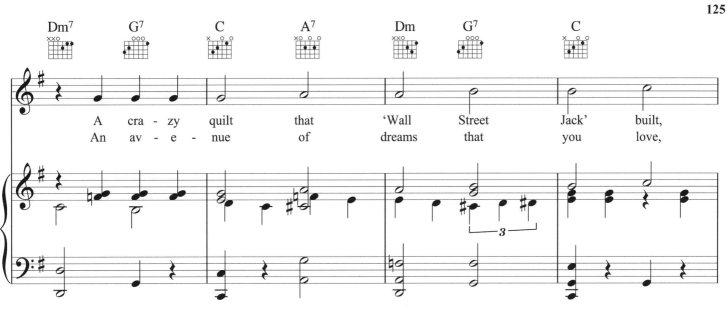

Hernando's Hideaway

from The Pajama Game

Words & Music by Richard Adler & Jerry Ross

fast em-brace,   it's called   Her-nan-do's   hide-a-way!   O - lay!

All   you see   are   sil-hou-ettes,   and   all   you hear   are

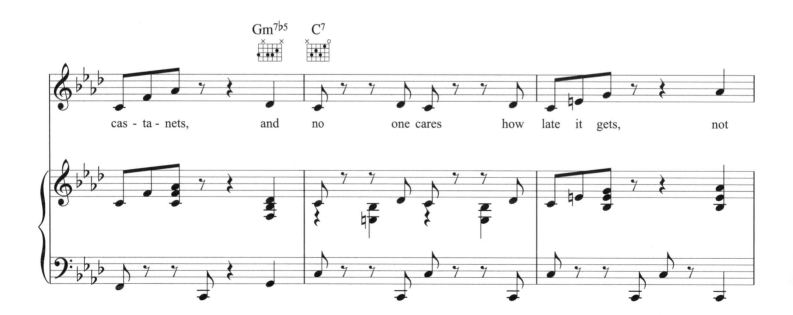

cas-ta-nets,   and   no   one cares   how   late it gets,   not

ev - 'ry - one you know.

But if you go to the spot that I am think- in' of, you will be free

to gaze at me and talk of love! Just

Happy Talk

from South Pacific

Words by Oscar Hammerstein II
Music by Richard Rodgers

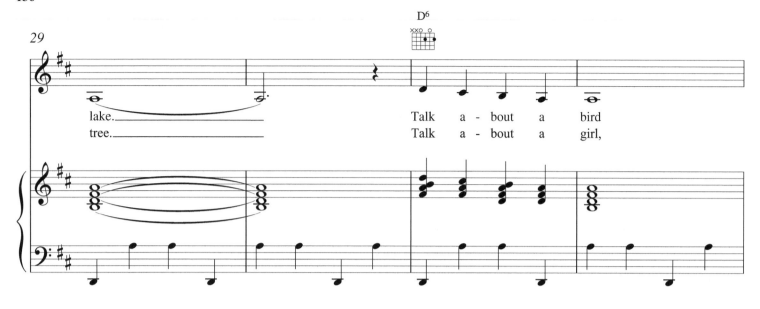

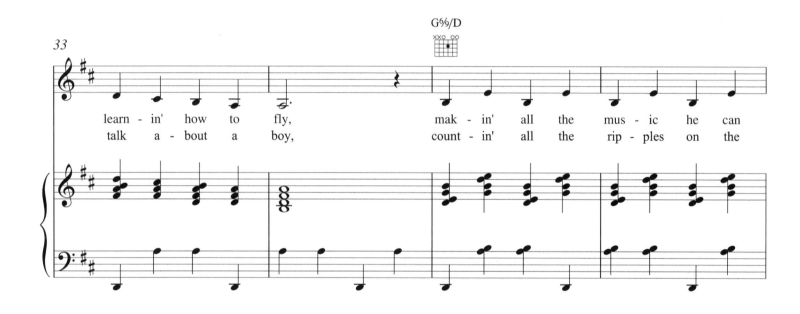

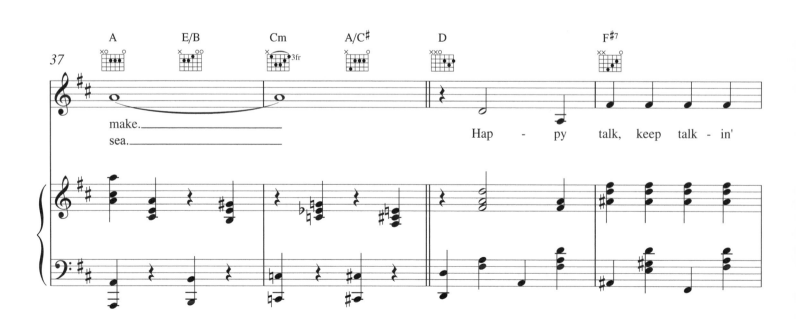

Tempo I°

Hello Dolly

from Hello Dolly

Words & Music by Jerry Herman

Hey There

from The Pajama Game

Words & Music by Richard Adler & Jerry Ross

Slowly and expressively

Hey there,_____ you with the stars in your eyes, love nev - er made a

fool of you, you used to be too wise!_____

Hopelessly Devoted To You

from Grease

Words & Music by John Farrar

I Don't Know How To Love Him

from Jesus Christ Superstar

Music by Andrew Lloyd Webber
Lyrics by Tim Rice

I don't know how to take this, I don't see why he moves me. He's a

man, he's just a man, and I've had so ma-ny

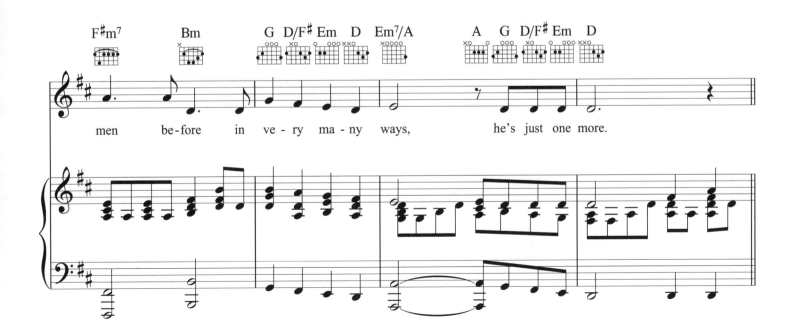

men be-fore in ve-ry ma-ny ways, he's just one more.

I should be in this po - si - tion. I'm the one who's al - ways been so
I'd be lost I'd be fright - ened. I could-n't cope, just could-n't cope. I'd

calm, so cool, no lov - er's fool, run - ning ev - 'ry
turn my head, I'd back a - way, I would-n't want to

To Coda ⊕

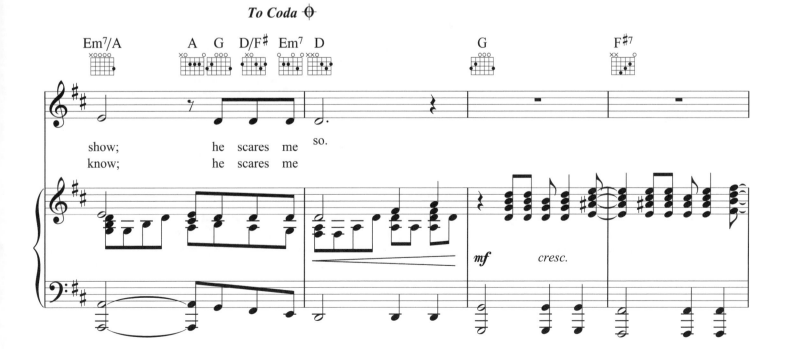

show; he scares me so.
know; he scares me

mf *cresc.*

I ne-ver thought I'd

D.S. al Coda

come to this,___ what's it all a - bout?_____

Coda

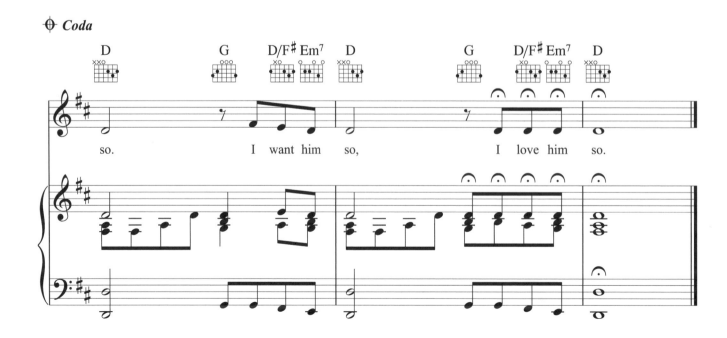

so. I want him so, I love him so.

If I Were A Rich Man

from Fiddler On The Roof

Words by Sheldon Harnick
Music by Jerry Bock

I Dreamed A Dream

from Les Misérables

Music by Claude-Michel Schönberg
Original Lyrics by Alain Boublil & Jean-Marc Natel
English Lyrics by Herbert Kretzmer

I prayed that God____ would be____ for - giv - ing.____

Then I was young and un - a - fraid,____

and dreams were made____ and used____ and was - ted.

There was no ran - som to be paid,____

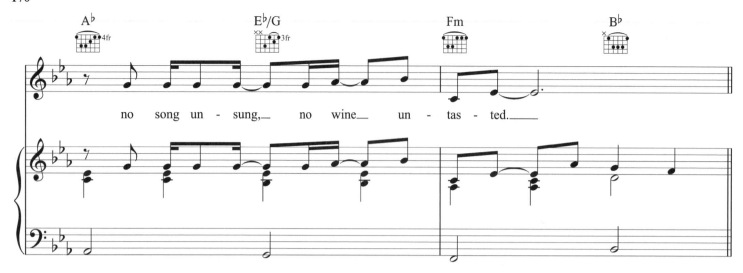

no song un - sung,___ no wine___ un - tas - ted.___

More movement

But the ti - gers come at night, with their voic - es soft as

thun - der,___ as they tear___ your hopes___ a -part,___

and they turn your dream to shame.

Broadly

Still I dream he'll come to me,

that we will live the years to - geth - er;

but there are dreams____ that can - not be,_____

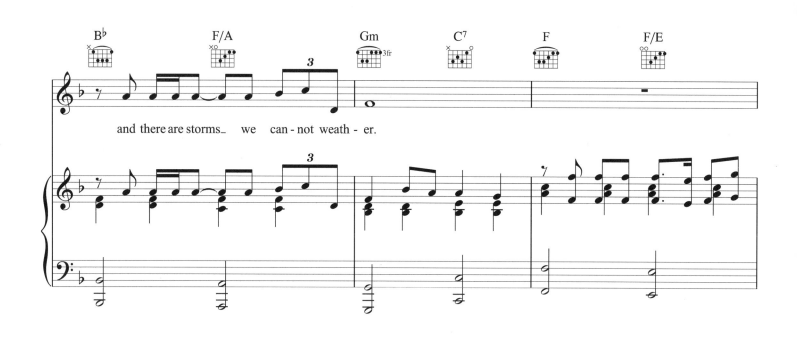

and there are storms__ we can - not weath - er.

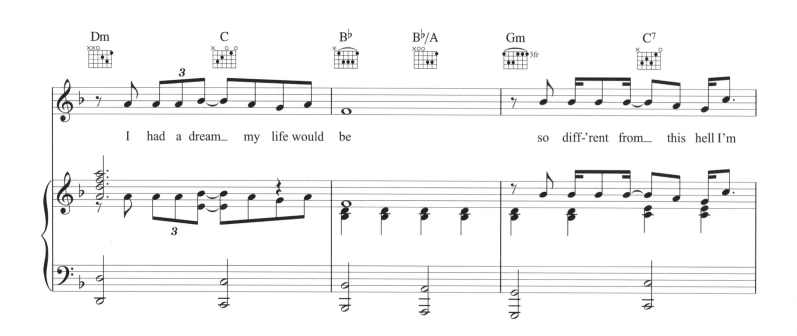

I had a dream__ my life would be   so diff-'rent from__ this hell I'm

liv - ing, so diff -'rent now from what it seemed,___

Slower

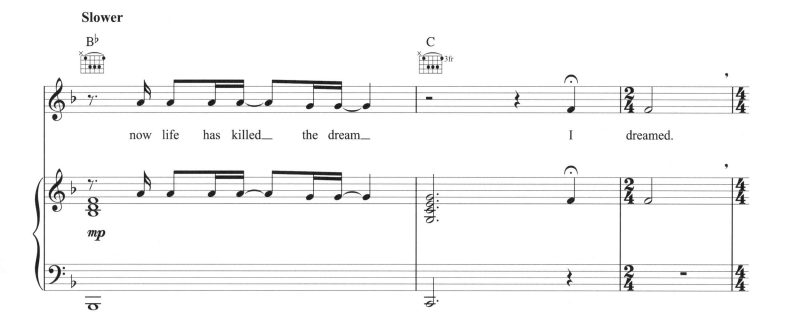

now life has killed___ the dream___ I dreamed.

rit. poco a poco

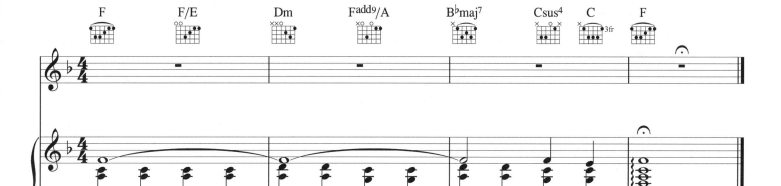

I Know Him So Well

from Chess

Words by Tim Rice
Music by Benny Andersson & Björn Ulvaeus

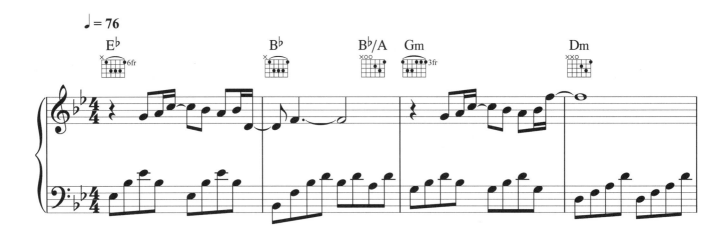

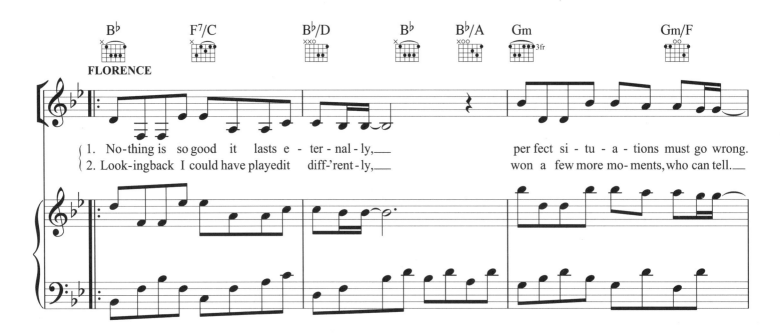

FLORENCE

1. No-thing is so good it lasts e - ter - nal - ly,____ per fect si - tu - a - tions must go wrong.
2. Look-ing back I could have played it diff - 'rent - ly,____ won a few more mo - ments, who can tell.____

If My Friends Could See Me Now

from Sweet Charity

Words by Dorothy Fields
Music by Cy Coleman

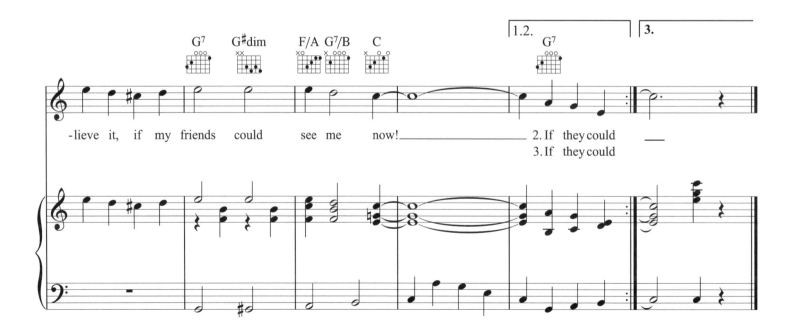

The Last Night Of The World

from Miss Saigon

Music by Claude-Michel Schönberg
Lyrics by Richard Maltby Jr. & Alain Boublil

a tempo I

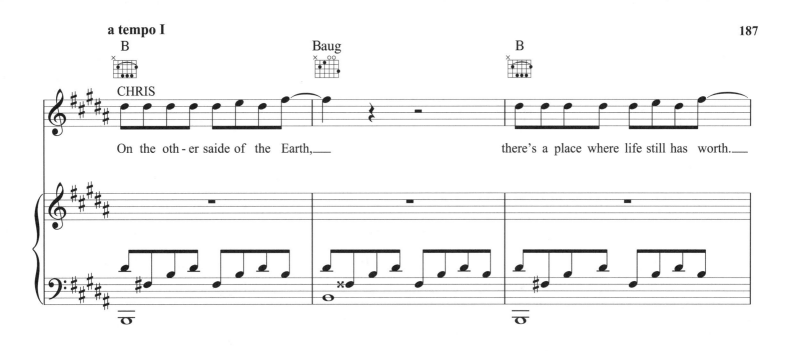

On the oth-er saide of the Earth,___ there's a place where life still has worth.___

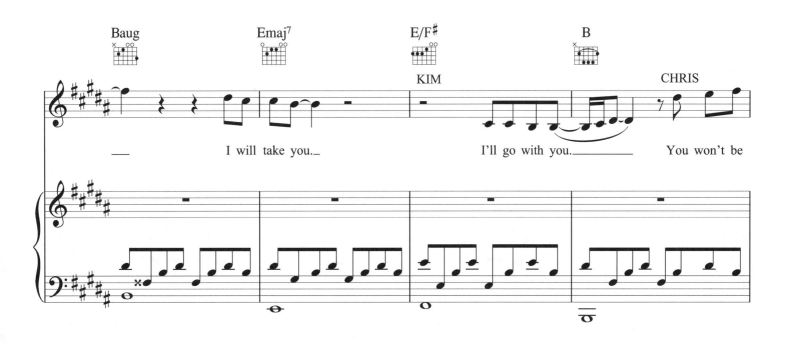

___ I will take you.__ I'll go with you.___ You won't be

poco più

-lieve all the things you'll see.___ I know 'cause you'll see them all with me.___

The Lambeth Walk

from Me And My Girl

Words by Douglas Furber & Arthur Rose
Music by Noel Gay

why don't you make your way there, go there, stay there. Once you get__ down Lam - beth way,__ ev - 'ry eve - ning, ev - 'ry day;__ you'll find your - self

1. do - in' the Lam - beth walk.

2. walk.

Losing My Mind

from Follies

Words & Music by Stephen Sondheim

1. The sun comes up, I think about you. The cof-fee cup, I think a-bout
2. The morn-ing ends, I think about you. I talk to friends, I think a-bout

you. I want you so, it's like I'm los-ing my mind.
you. And do they know? It's like I'm los-ing my mind.

and think a-bout you, spend sleep - less nights to think a-bout you. You said__ you loved

me, or were you just be-ing kind:___ or am I los-ing my mind?

I want__ you so,____ it's like I'm los-ing my mind.____

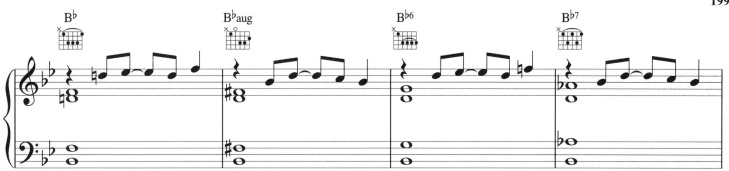

D.S. al Coda

Does no__ one know?__ It's like I'm los-ing my mind._____

⊕ *Coda*

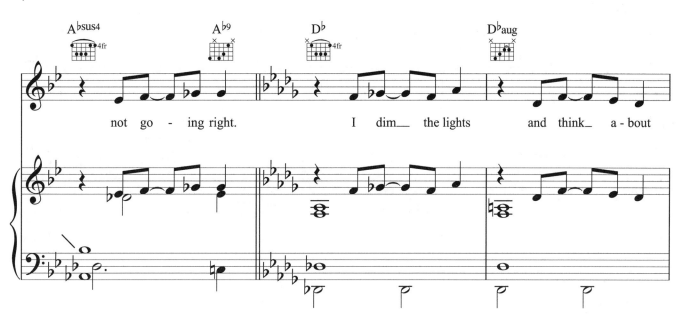

not go - ing right.   I dim__ the lights   and think_ a - bout

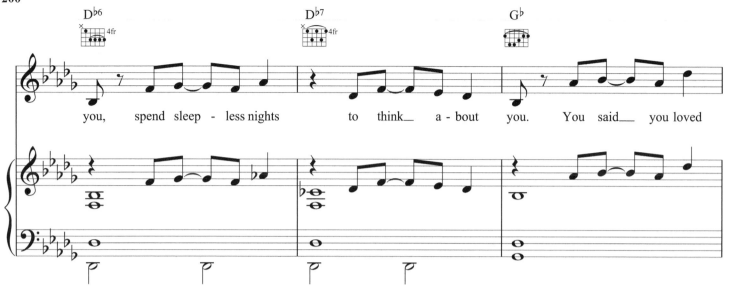

you, spend sleep - less nights to think___ a - bout you. You said___ you loved

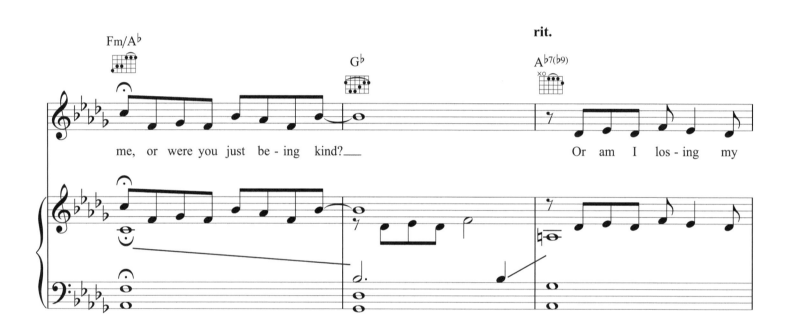

me, or were you just be - ing kind?___ Or am I los - ing my

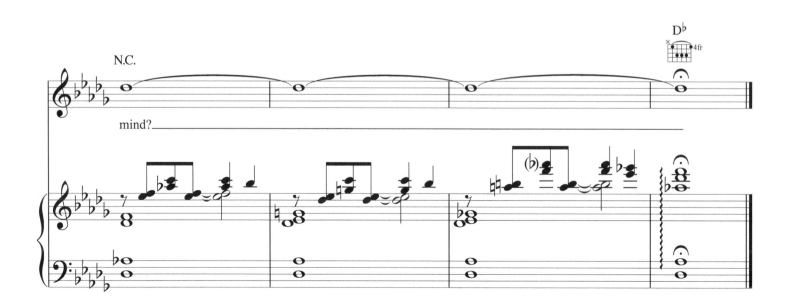

mind?___

Love Changes Everything

from Aspects Of Love

Music by Andrew Lloyd Webber
Lyrics by Don Black & Charles Hart

years. Love_____ bursts in and sud-den-ly, all our

wis-dom dis-ap-pears. Love_____ makes fools of

ev-'ry-one: all the rules we make are bro-ken. Yes

love,_____ love chan-ges ev-'ry-thing. Live or per-ish in its

Luck Be A Lady

from Guys And Dolls

Words & Music by Frank Loesser

yet be - fore this eve - ning is ov - er you might give me the brush.___ You

might for - get your man - ners, you might re - fuse to stay, and so the best that I can do is

pray.___

la - dy does-n't wan - der all ov - er the room and

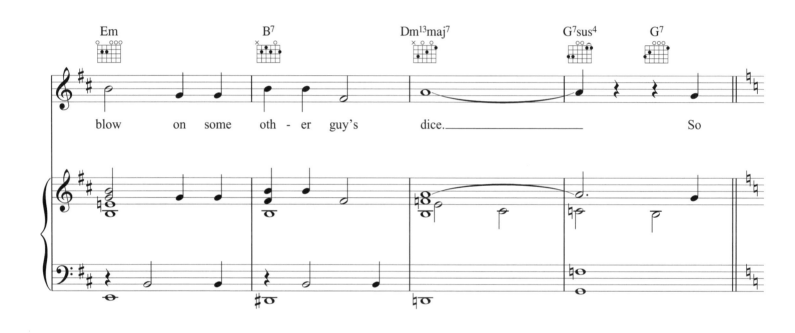

blow on some oth - er guy's dice._____ So

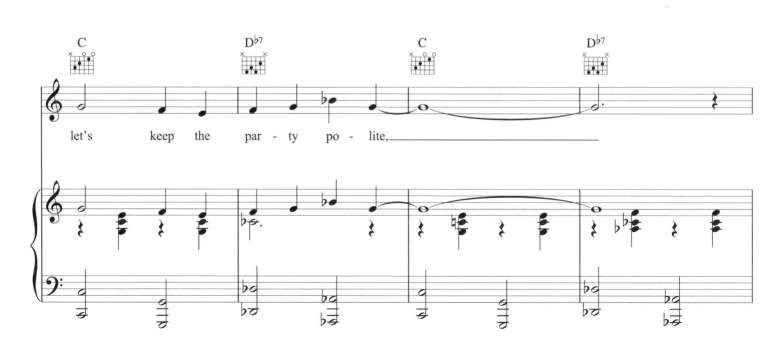

let's keep the par - ty po - lite,_____

luck be a la-dy, luck be a la-dy to-night.___

Nice Work If You Can Get It

from A Damsel In Distress

Words & Music by George Gershwin & Ira Gershwin

Mack The Knife

from The Threepenny Opera

Words by Bertolt Brecht
Music by Kurt Weill

The Music Of The Night

from The Phantom Of The Opera

Music by Andrew Lloyd Webber
Lyrics by Charles Hart
Additional Lyrics by Richard Stilgoe

PHANTOM
Night time sharp-ens, height-ens each sen-sa-tion;

dark-ness stirs and wakes im-ag-in-a-tion. Si-lent-ly the sens-es a-

-ban-don their de-fenc-es, help-less to re-sist the notes I write, for

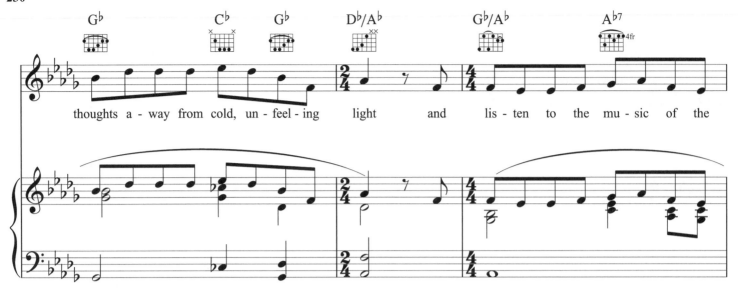

thoughts a - way from cold, un - feel - ing light and lis - ten to the mu - sic of the

night. Close your eyes and sur - ren - der to your

dark - est dreams! Purge your thoughts of the life you knew be -

rall.

Eb Eb7 Ab Ab7 Db

fore! Close your eyes, let your spi - rit start to soar and you'll

mp

rit. a tempo

Fm C F Db Ab/Db

live as you've nev - er lived be - fore. Soft - ly, deft - ly,

p

Db Ab/Db Db Ab/Db Gb Ab

mu - sic shall ca - ress you. Hear it, feel it, se - cret - ly po - sess you.

O - pen up your mind, let your fan - ta - sies un - wind in this

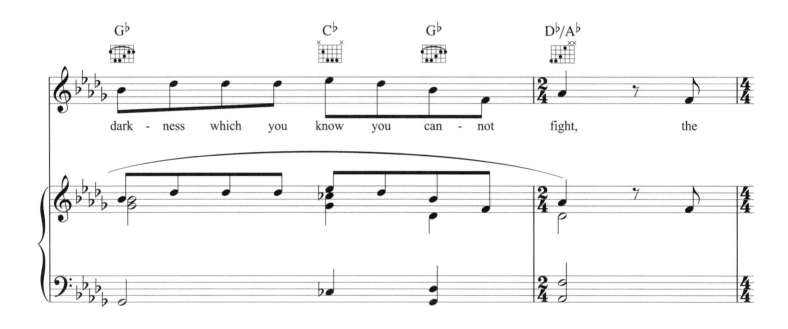

dark - ness which you know you can - not fight, the

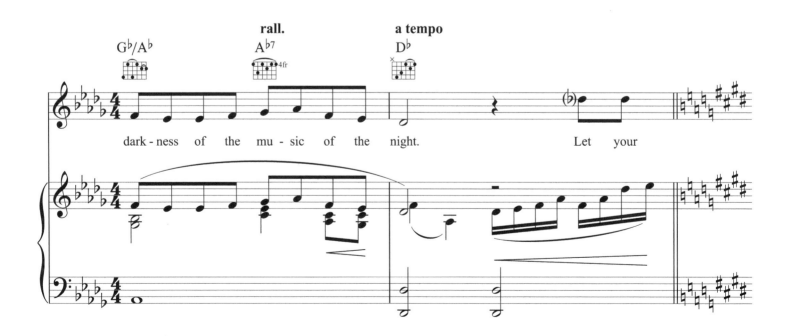

dark - ness of the mu - sic of the night. Let your

mind start a jour-ney through a strange, new world; leave all thoughts of the life you knew be-

-fore. Let your soul take you where you long to be! On-ly

then can you be-long to me. Float - ing, fall - ing, sweet in - tox - i - ca - tion.

My Favorite Things

from The Sound Of Music

Words by Oscar Hammerstein II
Music by Richard Rodgers

things.

Cream col - oured pon - ies and crisp ap - ple stru - dels;

door - bells and sleigh - bells and schnitz - el with nood - les; wild geese that

fly with the moon on their wings; these are a few of my

Oh, What A Beautiful Mornin'

from Oklahoma!

Words by Oscar Hammerstein II
Music by Richard Rodgers

1. There's a

bright gol - den haze on the mea - dow,
(2.) cat - tle are stand - ing like sta - tues.
(3.) sounds of the earth are like mu - sic.

—— there's a bright gol - den haze on the
—— All the cat - tle are stand - ing like
—— All the sounds of the earth are like

ev - 'ry - thing's go - ing my way.

2. All the
3. All the way.

Oh, what a beau - ti - ful day.

On My Own

from Les Misérables

Music by Claude-Michel Schönberg
Original French Lyrics by Alain Boublil & Jean-Marc Natel
English Lyrics by Herbert Kretzmer, Trevor Nunn & John Caird

And now I'm all a-lone a-gain; no-where to go, no-one to turn to.

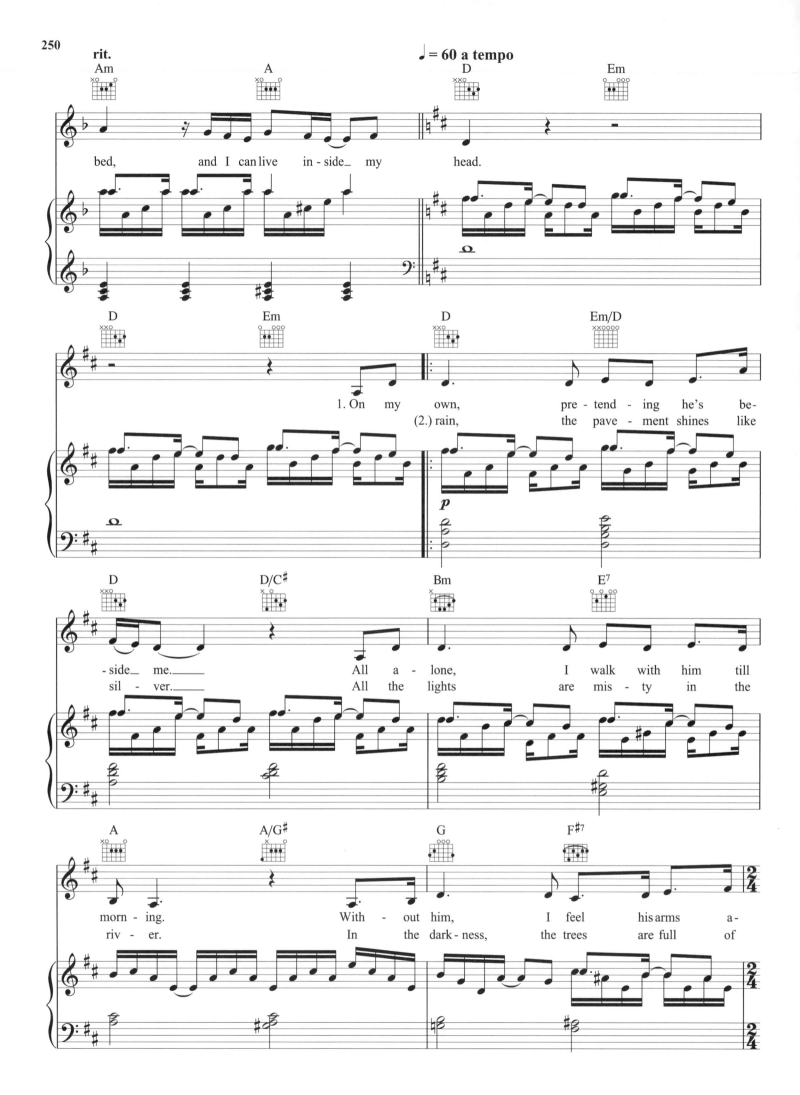

On The Street Where You Live

from My Fair Lady

Words by Alan Jay Lerner
Music by Frederick Loewe

is-n't there a gar-land all a-round that win-dow pane?

That could on-ly be your room!_____ This

street is like a gar-den and your door a gar-den gate, what a

love-ly place to wait. I have

One

from A Chorus Line

Words by Edward Kleban
Music by Marvin Hamlisch

Ol' Man River

from Showboat

Words by Oscar Hammerstein II
Music by Jerome Kern

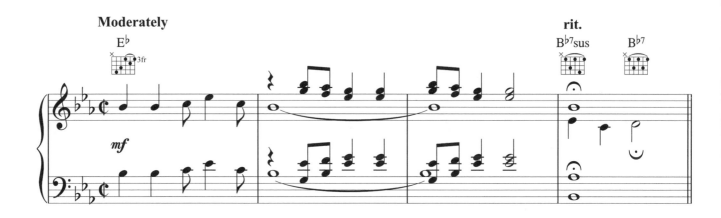

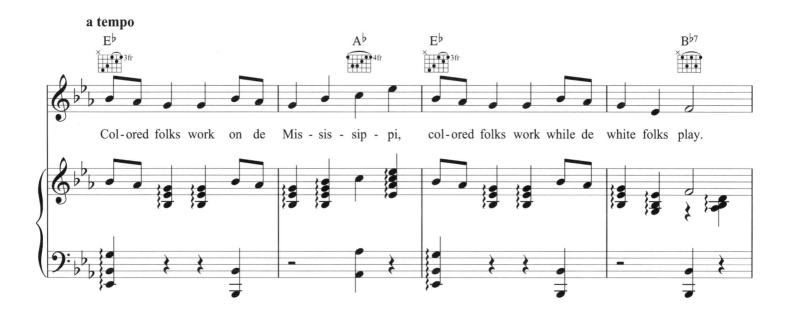

Col-ored folks work on de Mis - sis - sip - pi, col-ored folks work while de white folks play.

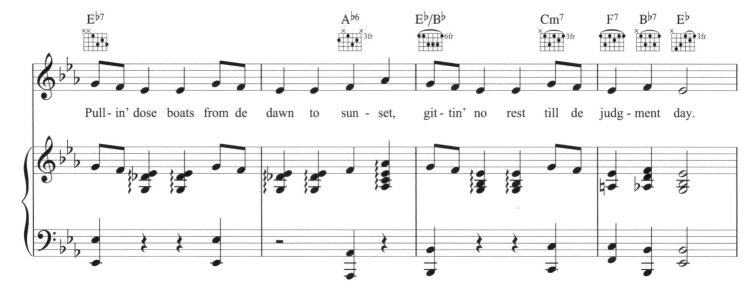

Pull-in' dose boats from de dawn to sun - set, git - tin' no rest till de judg - ment day.

Over The Rainbow

from The Wizard Of Oz

Words by E.Y. Harburg
Music by Harold Arlen

People

from Funny Girl

Words by Bob Merrill
Music by Jule Styne

Peo - ple, peo - ple who need peo - ple are the luck - i - est peo - ple in the world. We're

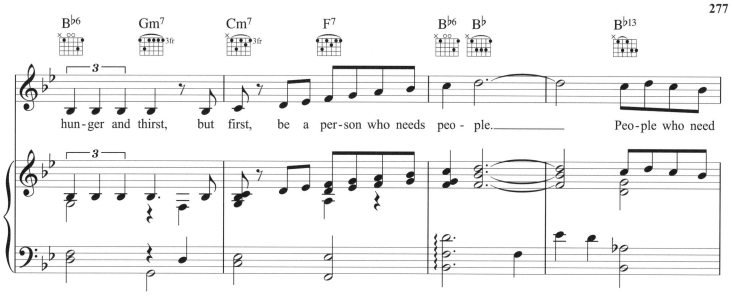

hun-ger and thirst, but first, be a per-son who needs peo - ple._____ Peo-ple who need

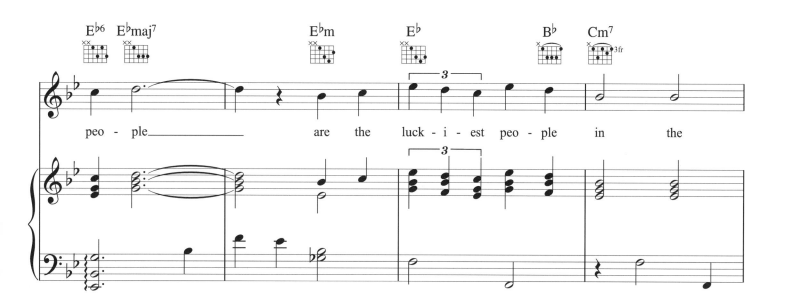

peo - ple_____ are the luck-i-est peo-ple in the

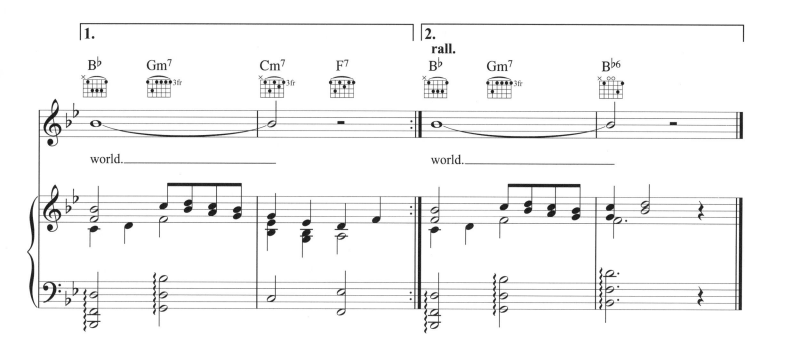

1.

world._____

2.
rall.

world._____

'S Wonderful

from Funny Face

Words & Music by George Gershwin & Ira Gershwin

Send In The Clowns

from A Little Night Music

Words & Music by Stephen Sondheim

This arrangement includes Mr Sondheim's revised lyrics for Barbra Streisand's recording.

Part Of Your World

from The Little Mermaid

Words by Howard Ashman
Music by Alan Menken

She Loves Me

from She Loves Me

Words by Sheldon Harnick
Music by Jerry Bock

Rubato

Well, well, well, well, well, well, well,

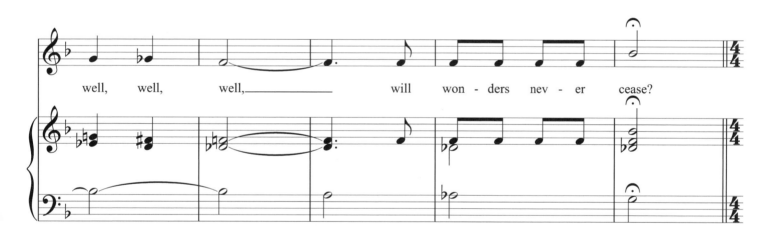

well, well, well,_____ will won - ders nev - er cease?

Moderately bright

She

Smoke Gets In Your Eyes

from Roberta

Words by Otto Harbach
Music by Jerome Kern

Summertime

from Porgy And Bess

Words & Music by George Gershwin, Ira Gershwin,
Dorothy Heyward & DuBose Heyward

Supercalifragilisticexpialidocious

from Mary Poppins

Words & Music by Richard M. Sherman & Robert B. Sherman

al - ways sound pre - co - cious: su - per - ca - li - fra - gi - lis - tic - ex - pi - al - i - do - cious!

1.

Um did - dle id - dle id - dle, um did - dle aye. Um did - dle id - dle id - dle, um did - dle aye.

Um did - dle id - dle id - dle, um did - dle aye. Um did - dle id - dle id - dle, um did - dle aye. (Boy) Be -

-cause I was a - fraid to speak when I was just a lad, me fath - er gave me nose a tweak and

Superstar

from Jesus Christ Superstar

Music by Andrew Lloyd Webber
Lyrics by Tim Rice

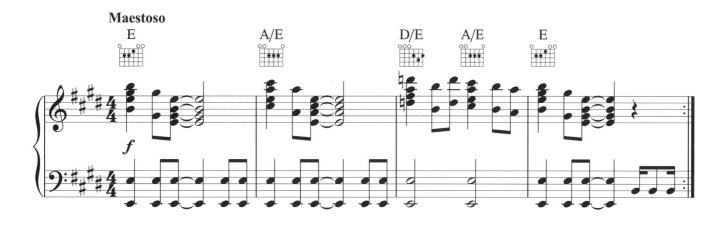

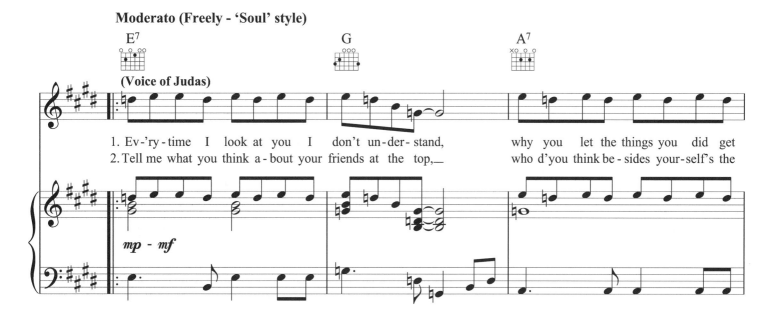

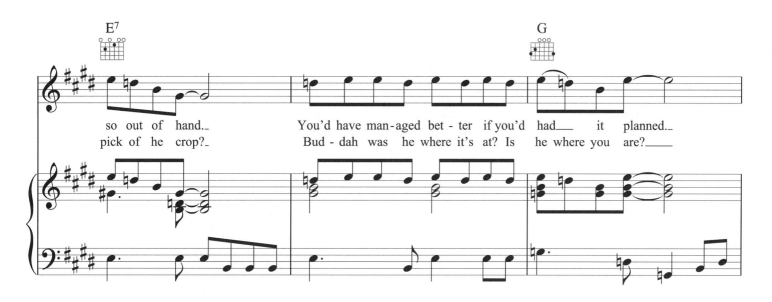

314

Take That Look Off Your Face

from Tell Me On A Sunday

Words by Don Black
Music by Andrew Lloyd Webber

There's No Business Like Show Business

from Annie Get Your Gun

Words & Music by Irving Berlin

grocer, the clerk get paid for what they do but no ap - plause._____ They'd
back aches, the flops, the sher - iff who es - corts you out of town._____ The
spot - light, the towns, your bag - gage with the la - bels past - ed on._____ The

glad - ly bid their drear - y jobs good - bye_____ for
open - ing when your heart beats like a drum,_____ the
saw - dust and the hors - es and the smell,_____ the

an - y - thing the - a - tri - cal, and why?_____ There's
clos - ing when the cus - tom - ers won't come._____ There's
towel you've tak - en from the last ho - tel._____ There's

Till There Was You

from The Music Man

Words & Music by Meredith Willson

love all a - round, but I nev - er heard it

sing - ing. No, I nev - er heard it at all till there was

1. you. And there was **2.** you.

Molto rit.

Top Hat White Tie And Tails

from Top Hat

Words & Music by Irving Berlin

A Whole New World

from Aladdin

Music by Alan Menken
Words by Tim Rice

Wilkommen

from Cabaret

Words by Fred Ebb
Music by John Kander

1. Will- kom - men! Bien - ve - nue!__ Wel- come!
2. (spoken ad lib.) *Meine damen und heren,* *mesdames et messieurs,* *Ladies und gentlemen:*

Frem - der, e - tran - ger, stran - ger.
Guten abend, *bon soir,* *good evening.*

You'll Never Walk Alone

from Carousel

Words by Oscar Hammerstein II
Music by Richard Rodgers

on through the wind, walk on through the

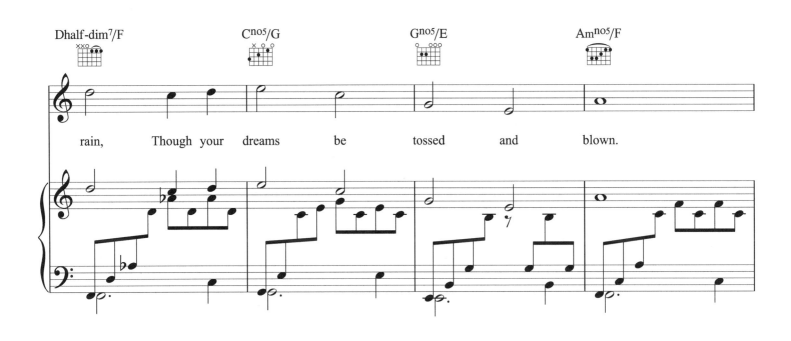

rain, Though your dreams be tossed and blown.

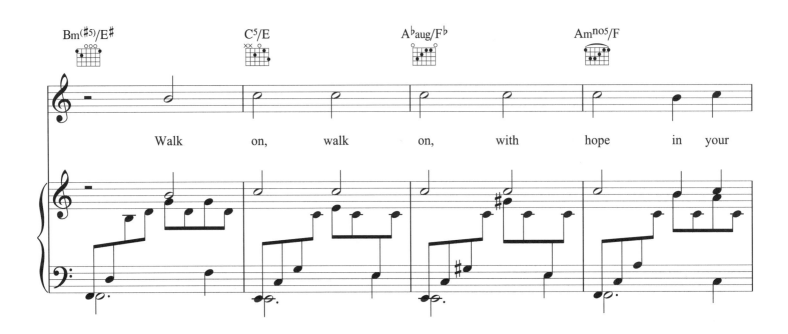

Walk on, walk on, with hope in your